THE ROAD

TO

PETRA

A SHORT ILLUSTRATED GUIDE
TO
EAST JORDAN

By

D. C. BARAMKI

Prof. of Ancient History, A. U. B.
Formerly Senior Archaeological Officer of the Palestine Government

Published by
ANTON NAZZAL & SONS
Proprietors : *Philadelphia Hotel, Amman, H. K. of Jordan*

9th. Edition — 1973
Completely revised

اهداء

الى حضرة صاحب الجلالة

الملك حسين بن طلال

ملك المملكة الاردنية الهاشمية

اطال الله بقاءه

صاحب الجلالة الهاشمية الملك الحسين المعظم

HIS MAJESTY KING HUSSEIN

FOREWORD

In preparing this short guide to the monuments of East Jordan, the author has relied to a large extent on his close acquaintance with the monuments of the country and its interesting past. The guide is intended primarily for casual visitors and tourists who have limited time at their disposal, and therefore only those sites which are easy of access have been included in the following narrative. For the more serious layman and scholar, a short bibliography is appended at the end of the text which may be profitably consulted.

East Jordan, like its western neighbour, is one of the Biblical Lands, and has always attracted the pious layman as well as the scholar. At present a number of sites is actually under excavation and our knowledge of the ancient culture and civilization of the country is increasing daily.

Since the appearance of the first edition in 1947, which went through several impressions, many changes have taken place. Places like Araq el Amir which were out of reach have since become easy of access and have been included in the present work.

The photographs in this guide are copyright by the Palestine Archaeological Museum in Jerusalem, the successor to the archives of the former Department of Antiquities in Palestine, and are published by kind permission of the Curator.

D. C. BARAMKI.

INTRODUCTION

To the First Edition

There has long been a demand from visitors to East Jordan for a book which will tell them something about the country in general, but so far this demand has remained unfulfilled. Now with the production of "The Road to Petra" the need is supplied, and Dr. Baramki gives a brief but comprehensive account of the country and its principal places of interest. His long experience in the Department of Antiquities of Palestine and his personal knowledge of all the sites of which he writes, place beyond doubt the accuracy of his statements, which are presented with a happy combination of scholarship and simplicity of language. It gives me much personal pleasure to see his little guide come into being, for in future instead of replying to questioners "No, nothing general has been written about East Jordan" I shall point to "The Road to Petra" and say "There you will find the answers to your question"). Mr. Nazzal of the Philadelphia Hotel is to be congratulated both on his foresight in publishing such a book and his choice of author.

G. LANKESTER HARDING
Department of Antiquities
AMMAN.

April, 1947

I. Topography and People of East Jordan

East Jordan comprises the Biblical Lands of Gilead, Ammon, Moab and Edom, and part of the desert to the east. It is bounded on the north by the River Yarmuk (Hieromax) and the Syrian Desert, on the east by Iraq and Saudi Arabia (along the west bank of Wadi Sirhan), on the south by Saudi Arabia and the Gulf of Aqaba, and on the west by the River Jordan, the Dead Sea, and the Wadi Araba in the Sinai Peninsula as far as the Gulf of Aqaba.

East Jordan consists of a flat range of mountains varying in height from 1,500 ft. to 4,500 ft. above sea level. The mountains merge on the east with the Syrian Desert, and on the west they are brought to an end abruptly by the Great Rift, of which the Jordan Valley, the Dead Sea, Wadi Araba and the Red Sea form a part. The mountain range is roughly divided into four parts (which correspond to the modern administrative districts, and to a certain extent, to the petty kingdoms of the Old Testament) by three perennial streams, flowing in steep and narrow gorges, viz, the Zerqa (Biblical Jabbok), the Mujib (Biblical Arnon) and the Wadi el Hasa (Biblical Zered). The District of Ajlun (Biblical Gilead) lies between the Yarmuk and the Zerqa; the District of Balqa (part of the Land of Moab which was wrested from the Moabites by the Amorites, and the Land of Ammonites to the east of it) lies between the Zerqa and the Mujib; the District of Kerak (the Land of Moab) lies between the Mujib and Wadi el Hasa; and the District of Ma'an (the Land of Edom and later of the Nabataeans) lies between Wadi el Hasa and the Gulf of Aqaba.

In addition to these main streams, other less important wadis cross the country from east to west like Wadi Shu'aib Zerqa Ma'in, Wadi Wala and Wadi Musa. The Jordan Valley is irrigated by the waters of some of these streams and by numerous springs. The mountain range to the east relies to a great extent on rain water for its cultivation, with a few small springs here and there contributing their small but welcome share to the scanty rainfall of Jordan. The area under cultivation embraces more or less that part of Jordan lying west of the present railway line; the rest of the country is barren desert.

East Jordan has not been properly surveyed, but its area has been estimated at over 20,000 sq. miles. Its population has been variously estimated at 1,000,000 to 1,200,000 souls. The bulk of the population is Moslem Arab, but in addition there are some 150,000 Christian Arabs, belonging mainly to the Greek Orthodox Church, with small Roman Catholic, Melkite and Anglican communities in the principal towns, and about 10,000 Moslem Circassians and Chechens, descendants of those who were settled by the Turkish Sultan Abdul Hamid in certain parts of Jordan after the Russo-Turkish War of 1877-78 when some parts of the Caucasus were ceded to Russia.

East Jordan was, until quite recently, a strictly agricultural and pastoral country; but under the sound direction of its young monarch and the wise policy of his ministers, the country has made great strides towards industrialization. A great spurt of building activity was launched with the accession of the present King, while the tobacco industry, the phosphate industry and many others have been greatly developed, and the country is at present able to dispense with many commodities which it had to import in the past, but is now producing in sufficient quantities for local consumption.

One of the principal trades to which the country is paying particular attention is the tourist traffic. New first class roads have been built which link up the principal cities and make access to the important monuments easy, and a number of comfortable hotels have been put up to accommodate the increasing volume of tourists.

II. Outline of the History of East Jordan

The ancient history of East Jordan is closely linked with that of West Jordan, Phoenicia and Syria, and like the history of these countries it embraces periods of great activity and progress, punctuated by other periods of obscurity when the country was overrun by marauding nomads from the Syrian Desert.

Archaeological exploration and excavations have revealed that the desert, as well as the fertile area of East Jordan, was occupied by man very early in the Stone Age, a fact which demonstrates that water existed in the now barren desert in that remote period. Primitive man has left his imprint on the desert in the form of worked flints discovered at various Old Stone Age stations.

Village life first started during the New Stone Age, and remains of some of the ancient villages have been discovered in various parts of the country in recent years. Surface exploration and excavation have revealed that urbanization on a limited scale made its appearance during the Third Millennium B.C.

This civilization after flourishing for six centuries was brought to an end by the onslaught of the Amorites, a large wave of Semites who invaded Phoenicia, Syria and East and West Jordan during the Twenty Third Century B.C. at a time when Egypt had become so weak under the pharaohs of the Seventh and Eighth Dynasties as a result of the rise of feudalism in the country, that she was unable to defend her neighbours.

Over the ruins of the former civilization, a new civilization arose during the Second Millennium B.C. when Egypt revived her former glory under the pharaohs of the

Twelfth Dynasty. New cities arose in East Jordan, industry revived and trade flourished.

In recent years, the theory has been advanced that Transjordan lapsed into nomadism about the Sixteenth Century B.C. and was relatively empty. This theory is based on the absence of potsherds belonging to the Sixteenth to Thirteenth Centuries B.C. on the surface of most of the ruins and artificial mounds in Jordan. However a chance discovery at the airport in Amman and the excavations at Deir Alla, Irbid and other places have shown that the country was by no means empty but that it was occupied by civilized folk during that period in question. Furthermore, as has already been pointed out, our knowledge of the early pottery of East Jordan is still in its infancy and some of the potsherds claimed to belong to the Twelfth Century and later may actually belong to the Fourteenth and Thirteenth Centuries B.C.

East Jordan first comes into History with the arrival of the Israelites after their captivity in Egypt, and their long wanderings in the wilderness. Prior to that, mention may be made of the Biblical story of Chedorlaomer, King of Elam, who with others, attacked the Kings of Sodom and Gomorrah, and the story of the destruction of these latter places in Lot's days (Gen. xiv and xix, 23). The late Jesuit Father Mallon, who carried out excavations at Tuleilat al Ghassul at the north end of the Dead Sea, has suggested the identification of this site with Sodom and Gomorrah, but with inconclusive evidence.

The Israelites, coming from the south, first encountered the Edomites, whose dominion extended as far north as Wadi el Hasa (River Zered); they had previously dispossessed the Horites, or Hurrians, who probably settled in Jordan from the Eighteenth to the Fourteenth Centuries B.C. and occupied the land in their stead. The Edomites refused the Israelites' permission to pass through their land (Numbers xx 14-21), thus forcing them to make a great detour through Aqaba and the desert in order to reach the Arnon, the north boundary of the reduced Land of Moab, which with its capital at Kir-Haraseth (II Kings iii 25 modern Kerak), extended from the River Zered on the south to the Arnon on the north. North of Moab lay the Land of the Amorites, which stretched from the Arnon to the Jabbok, ruled at the time by King Sihon. This land previously belonged to the Moabites but was wrested from them by the Amorites. King Sihon contested the passage of the Israelites through his land and was signally defeated by them. The Israelites then pushed their arms further north and dispossessed Og, King of Bashan, of his land. Moses next turned his attention to Moab, and captured it from the Moabites. Transjordan was allotted to the children of Reuben, Gad and half the tribe of Manasseh. From Mt. Nebo in Moab, Moses was allowed a glimpse of the Promised Land, which he was destined never to enter.

After completing the occupation of Palestine, David turned his attention to East Jordan. Moab was again attacked and crushed; Ammon, after a lengthy siege of its capital Rabbath-Ammon (Amman), was similarly routed; and Edom, which had been spared by the Israelites so far, was annihilated with great slaughter. However Ammon, Moab and Edom were able later to regain their independence and Mesha, King of Moab, was able to avenge the wrong inflicted on his country by Omri, by dealing his son Ahab a crushing blow. This feat he recorded on the famous "Moabite Stone" which was found at Diban, and is now in the Louvre Museum in Paris.

During the Assyrian Period of ascendancy from the Ninth to the Seventh Centuries B.C., the kings of Moab, Edom and Ammon threw in their lot on several occasions with that of Merodach Baladan, the claimant to the Babylonian throne, and later intrigued with the Egyptian pharaohs. They suffered severely for their incalcitrance on every occasion. They continued to pay tribute to Assyria until the sack of Nineveh and the downfall of the Assyrian Empire (612 B.C.), when their masters changed and instead of paying tribute to the lords of Nineveh, they became vassals of the Chaldaean Kings of Babylon. But the picture remained essentially the same, frequent revolts followed by harsh reprisals.

A period of peace was enjoyed under the Achaemaenid Dynasty of Persia. The Persian satraps maintained law and order and gave an opportunity to the Nabataeans to start playing their important role in the history of East Jordan. Little is known about the Nabataeans before 312 B.C. They are first mentioned as paying tribute to the Assyrians about 650 B.C. From the earliest times they appear to have been engaged in trade, and as soon as they were firmly established in and around Petra, they devoted their energies to maintaining that trade, which was to become the source of their prosperity, and to protect the trade routes of the ancient East. They were in a favourable position geographically to do so, for their territory lay astride the ancient trade routes from the south and east to Egypt and Syria. Great profits accrued to the Nabataeans from the fees they charged for transporting and guarding merchandise; this wealth is reflected in the imposing monuments they bequeathed to posterity at Petra "the rose red city", and the great number of ruined forts which they built elsewhere in East Jordan in order to protect the frontier, and forcibly to divert trade to their capital. From 312 B.C. to 106 A.D. the Nabataeans were firmly established around the Gulf of Aqaba and in the Negeb, the land formerly occupied by the Edomites. Antigonus Monophthalmos captured Petra in 312 B.C. and carried away a great treasure, but his army was waylaid by the Nabataeans in a night attack and completely annihilated. The Nabataeans later took advantage of the turmoil resulting from the frequent wars between the Seleucids and the Ptolemies to expand their territory, and consolidate their position, retiring when prudence and necessity required to their capital Petra, secure within its rocky fastnesses, beyond the three narrow passes through which only, could it be approached. By the Second Century B.C. the Nabataeans had extended their territory up to the Arnon, thus absorbing the ancient land of both Edom and Moab. In 169 B.C. during the reign of Aretas, the Nabataeans were deemed by Jason, the Jewish High Priest, to be sufficiently strong as to be able to afford him shelter, when he was fleeing from the wrath of the Seleucids; this protection was however refused. Under el Hareth II (Aretas II Erotimus, 110-96 B.C.), the Nabataeans had become sufficiently powerful to create a vast empire spreading over an extensive area. They waged war on the Maccabaeans, and in 90 B.C., under Obedas I inflicted a heavy defeat on Alexander Jannaeus. During the reign of el Hareth III (Aretas III, 85-60 B.C.) they reached the zenith of their power; they defeated Antiochus XII, who fell in battle, occupied Syria and captured Damascus, where they minted coins. However a more formidable foe appeared on the horizon during this king's reign, who was destined eventually to bring the Nabataean kingdom tottering to its knees; the mighty arm of Rome reached Transjordan, and the city on the Tiber became henceforth the arbiter of all disputes in the Near East. Aretas, coming to the assistance of his ally John Hyrcanus, in order to help in the siege of Aristobulus in Jerusalem, was ordered by Scaurus, Pompey's general, to withdraw, whereupon Aristobulus attacked and dealt him a heavy blow. Pompey's subsequent march on Petra however had to be abandoned, and Scaurus was bought off from following it up with a second attack. A third march under Gabinius, during the reign of the Nabataean King Obedas II, did not achieve anything. The fate of the Nabataeans, from now on, lay in the balance, and they became involved willy nilly in the affairs of Rome in the Near East. Malchus I thought it prudent to send a force of calvary to Caesar during the Alexandrian War, although later he refused to give refuge to Herod when in 40 B.C. the Parthians occupied Palestine.

El Hareth IV (Aretas IV, 9 B.C. - A.D. 40) sent a contingent against the Jews to help Varus, though later he waged war on Rome's ally Herod Antipas, his son-in-law, for divorcing his daughter. It was this same Aretas who was ruling Damascus when St. Paul escaped there. During his reign the Nabataeans' dominions extended from the Euphrates to the Red Sea. The Romans tolerated this state of affairs so long as it suited their purpose, and because it had the advantage of keeping the wild desert tribes in order; but later, in A.D. 106 during the reign of Malchus III, they suppressed the Nabataean Kingdom and added it to the Province of Arabia.

Concurrently, with the expansion of the Nabataean domains from the Third to the First Centuries B.C., the Decapolis came into being. This was a confederation of ten cities, to which others were added later, lying on both sides of the Jordan. They were modelled on Greek cities, spoke the Greek language, practised the Greek religion, and adopted Greek culture. Some of these cities like Pella (Khirbat el Fahl), Dion and Gerasa (Jerash) were probably founded by the soldiers of Alexander or of his generals; others like Scythopolis (Beisan), Philadelphia (Amman), Gadara (Umm Qeis), Raphana, Kanatha (Kanawat in Jebel ed Druse), Hippos (Fik in Syria) and Damascus were older cities in which Greek communities settled, at the same time expanding and embellishing them. Soon after the arrival of Pompey in Palestine in 64 B.C., they formed a military alliance, with his consent, for self-protection against the Jews and the Nabataeans alike, and the trepidation of the wild desert tribes. When later Trajan joined Peraea with the Decapolis to create the Province of Arabia (to which the Nabataean kingdom was added later) these cities retained some measure of their autonomous status.

Herod the Great held Peraea, i.e. that part of East Jordan roughly between the Arnon and the Decapolis. It was at the fortress of Machaerus (Muqawer) which was built by Alexander Jannaeus to guard the frontier against the Nabataeans that Herod Antipas, the tetrarch, slew John the Baptist (Matthew xiv 3-12).

East Jordan was organized under Roman rule as it had never been before. A stop was put to desert raids and petty feuds. The arts of peace flourished, new towns were built, and the old expanded. To this period belongs the greatness of Jerash.

Christianity gained a strong foothold in Transjordan between the Second and the Third Centuries A.D. During the reign of Justinian many churches were built at Jerash, Madaba, and elsewhere, and the country enjoyed a period of peace except for the desert area between the Land of the Ghassanids, who lived on the fringes of Jordan in a state of hired mercenaries to the Byzantine Emperors, and the Lakhmids of Hira, the Arab buffer state west of the Persian Empire of the Sassanians. Chosroes II of Persia conquered the country in A.D. 614 thereby disorganizing its defences and prepared it for the coming onslaught of the Arabs in A.D. 635. East Jordan was occupied by the Arabs immediately after the Battle of Yarmuk.

The desert of East Jordan was very popular with the Umayyads, the First Dynasty in Islam, and they left their mark on it in the numerous palaces with which the desert is dotted. East Jordan remained in Arab occupation enjoying a period of peace and somewhat insignificant prosperity, until this was disturbed by the Crusaders. Under the Crusaders, the Principality of Transjordan (Outre Jourdain) was the most important fief of the Latin Kingdom of Jerusalem with its capital at Le Krak or La Pierre de Desert (Kerak). Fortresses were built at Kerak, Shobak (Montreal), Wadi Musa (Le Val de Moise), and Jeziret Far'on, the small island of Aqaba (Graye). From these different fortresses the Crusaders used to sally forth and attack the Moslem caravans plying between Damascus, Mecca, and Egypt sometimes, even, in violation of current treaties or truces. (As Renaud de Chatillon did; for this act of bad faith he lost his life when he was taken prisoner at the Battle of Hattin). One of Saladin's generals built Qal'at er Rabad, above Ajlun, in order to harass the Crusaders, and to protect his caravans.

After the Crusaders, East Jordan reverted slowly to obscurity and tribal raids, except for the short periods when the Mameluke rulers of Egypt saw fit to impose their authority on the country, or to carry on their family feuds there.

The Great War of 1914-18 brought with it great changes. East Jordan became the field of Lawrence's activities. Soon after the country's liberation from the Turks, King Abdullah (then Amir) assumed the administration of the country under the aegis of the British Administration in Palestine. Thanks to His Majesty's benevolent rule, and the wise administration of his able ministers, the country has progressed considerably; peace and security have been established, tribal raids have ceased and the Bedu have learnt the advantages of a peaceful occupation, almost unknown during the former Turkish Period. In

May 1946, East Jordan was proclaimed independent and the former Amir Abdullah became its first king.

In 1949 after the termination of the Mandate in Palestine, and in response to an appeal by the people of Arab Palestine, the section of Palestine retained by the Arabs was united with Transjordan to form the new Hashemite Kingdom of Jordan. The Arab Legion played a prominent role in the Arab Jewish War and helped to curb Zionist ambitions. King Abdullah was succeeded in 1951 by King Talal, who abdicated in favour of his son, the present King Hussein, in 1952. The country may well look forward to further progress and prosperity under the guidance of its new king, who has already demonstrated great ability and political acumen and has converted the country into a flourishing and progressive state.

III. The Monuments of East Jordan.
Jerusalem to Amman.

In order to gain admisssion to Jordan a valid passport is necessary, visa-ed by a Jordan Consul abroad.

To visit the principal monuments of East Jordan nine days are required: a day for Amman and Araq el Amir, a day for Jerash, four days for Petra and Aqaba including the journey there and back, a day for Madaba and the neighbouring sites, a day for the Umayyad Palaces in the desert and a day for Umm Jimal. Persons pressed for time may omit the last four sites.

For travellers coming from Europe, North Africa and the United States, there are two possible routes to Jordan, either by air from Beirut, Cairo or Nicosia direct to Amman or Jerusalem, or by car from Beirut via Damascus. Travellers landing in Jerusalem can proceed directly to Amman by car.

The journey from Jerusalem to Amman via Jericho and Allenby Bridge is 107 Kilometres, while the journey from Jerusalem to Amman via the Dead Sea and Na'our is only 88 Kilometres. The journey via Allenby Bridge takes normally from 2½ to 3 hours, including short stops on the way. Leaving Jerusalem at about 8 a.m., it should be possible for one to reach Amman in time for lunch, even if the trip up to Jebel Yusha' is undertaken.

Taking the first alternative route, one crosses the Jordan at Allenby Bridge. The road thence to Amman is well metalled, and runs close to Wadi Nimrin (the Biblical "waters of Nimrin"). At the village of Shunet Nimrin, 54 Kms. from Amman, the climb up Wadi Shu'eib commences. Shu'eib, after whom the Wadi is called, is the

Biblical Jethroe, Moses' father-in-law. This village is the headquarters of the strong Adwan tribe.

A visit to Tell Kufrein, 5 Kms. south of Shunet Nimrin, is recommended to those travellers who are not pressed for time. It is the traditional site of the Biblical Abel Shittim where "Israel abode" before crossing the Jordan (Numbers xxvi 1).

Half a kilometre beyond Shunet Nimrin to the right of the bridge, there are rock cut caves which formed part of a Byzantine monastery of the Fourth to Sixth Centuries. A little beyond near Km. 48 along the metalled road to Amman, the field gun, with which the Turks shelled Jericho in 1919, can be seen at the bottom of the valley. As one proceeds up the picturesque wadi, flanked by oleander bushes, the country is wild and barren in parts, and rich in vegetation in others. After crossing the bridge near Km. 38 from Amman, the ascent up the wadi becomes very steep and the country very wild. In former days it was not an uncommon sight in the sweltering heat of July or August to see an eagle carrying a snake in its beak or claws flying over the rocky hills. The ascent breaks a few miles before we reach es Salt, where the top of the plateau is reached and we start driving past the rich terraced vineyards of that town, which are famous all over the Near East.

Es Salt was the chief city of the Belqa, until it was superseded by Amman. The population is about 25,000, 15,000 of whom are Moslems and the rest Christians mainly Greek Orthodox. It is situated on the slopes of a few terraced hills on one of which stands the ruined fortress built in 1220 by the Mameluk Sultan al Malik al Mu'azzam, destroyed by the Mongols and refortified by the Mameluk Sultan Beybars in 1261. Although devoid of important monuments, a stop of one hour here is well rewarded by the view obtained from the top of

Jebel Yusha', 3,600 ft. above sea level north of the town. The whole of the Jordan Valley and the hills beyond as far north as Mt. Hermon in Syria lie at one's feet. The shrine on top of the hill is the tomb of the Prophet Hosea (Yusha' in Arabic), according to Moslem tradition.

Suweileh, 12 Kms. before Amman, is one of the Circassian villages founded by Sultan Abdul Hamid in 1878. Amman is reached after crossing the plateau beyond Suweileh, where megalithic remains can be seen, and then descending into the city, built at the confluence of Wadi Zerqa and Wadi Amman.

The second route via Na'our is shorter, more comfortable but less picturesque. After crossing the bridge over the Jordan, the road rises steeply towards the plateau. A short distance beyond the Jordan, there is a track leading to Tuleilat el Ghassul, a site which was occupied during the Fourth Millennium B.C.

A short distance before reaching Amman, we come to Na'our, one of the Circassian villages, founded by Sultan Abdul Hamid.

Travellers flying direct to Amman can proceed with the programme outlined on the following pages.

AMMAN

Amman (Rabbath-Ammon, Philadelphia) is the capital of Jordan; it has a population of over 300,000 souls, mostly Moslem. It is the residence of the King, the seat of the Government of Jordan and the hub of the country's life. Alone of all the cities in East Jordan it boasts of a very fine hotel, the Philadelphia, which makes it a suitable centre from which to start excursions to the different monuments of the country.

Main landmarks in the history of Amman.

1200 B.C.	Rabbath-Ammon mentioned in the Old Testament as the capital of the Ammonites and as containing the iron bed of Og, King of Bashan.
1000 B.C.	Captured by David. It was during the siege of this town that David had Uriah the Hittite placed in the forefront of attack in order to bring about his death so as to be able to appropriate for himself Uriah's wife the beautiful Bath-Sheba.
1000-700 B.C.	Vassal of the North Kingdom of Israel or of the Kingdom of Judah by turn, depending on whoever was the stronger.
700-600 B.C.	Vassal of Assyria.
600-539 B.C.	Vassal of Babylonia.
285-247 B.C.	Hellenized by Ptolemy Philadelphos.
63 B.C.	Joined the Decapolis.
31 B.C.	Occupied by the Nabataeans, but soon liberated by Herod on behalf of the Romans.
A.D. 90	Absorbed in the new Roman Province of Arabia.

ROMAN THEATRE — AMMAN

A.D. 350   Became the seat of a bishopric.

A.D. 634-1877 Insignificant and partly in ruins.

A.D. 1878   Settled with Circassians by Sultan Abdul Hamid.

A.D. 1922   Became the capital of the new state of Jordan.

The monuments of Amman are few and can be visited in a single day. Most of the imposing ones go back to the Antonine Period. Facing the Philadelphia is the large Roman Theatre, the seats of which are built against the slope in the hollow of the hill, with a seating capacity for 4000 spectators. The vaults under some of the seats were used to help in ushering the spectators to

Jordanian Army Officer from loyalist tribesmen

their seats, although there is an alternative theory that they were the place where the animals or gladiators were kept prior to entering the small arena, now indicated by the row of columns facing the theatre. The seat of honour is in the middle of the top row.

Next to the hotel, on the east side, is a smaller theatre commonly misnamed the Odeon, while to the west was the Forum, of which nothing remains now.

Overlooking the town on the north and east, is the Acropolis (Qala'a), built on a plateau surrounded by valleys on all sides except the north where an escarpment was specially cut to complete the isolation of the fortress. It was enclosed in a wall built of large stones, which can still be traced, fortified by towers at each corner.

The entrance, which is on the south, leads into a spacious open court in the middle of which stand the ruins

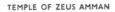

TEMPLE OF ZEUS AMMAN

of a temple, which in all probability was dedicated to Zeus (or to Hercules as some would have it); only the lower courses exist at present; but in addition there are two large columns, fallen to the ground, fragments of a cornice and an inscribed lintel dating the temple to the reign of the Emperor Marcus Aurelius (A.D. 161-180). These are all that remains of what was once a magnificent temple.

North of the temple lie the remains of another structure, planned in the form of a square enclosing a cross. It is known locally as "el Qasr", the castle. From the decoration of the interior, it appears that this monument was the work of either one of the Ghassanid Kings or more likely one of the Umayyad Caliphs of Damascus. It is built against a Roman atrium, belonging to the temple north of it, which extends the whole width of the Acropolis, and which has an apse at the north and a spacious atrium at the south. A new Museum of Antiquities has been built at the south end of the Qala. A visit to this is essential for obtaining a cross section of the culture of East Jordan over the ages.

For those who are able to spend more than one day at Amman a visit to the ruins in the centre of the city is recommended. The Mosque of Amman was originally an Abbasid structure which was renovated in 1924. An exedra belonging to an ancient Nymphaeum or possibly a bath can be seen near the mosque close to the confluence of the two wadis. It is now obscured from view by modern buildings.

Among the modern monuments of Amman mention may be made of Qasr Raghdan, the King's palace, to the southeast of the city, and the royal palaces at Jabal Amman.

A visit to Araq el Amir is strongly recommended for visitors to Amman. It is situated a short distance from the village of Wadi Sir set within a deep valley. Taking the Wadi Sir road which starts from the main square of the town, one reaches the village in less than twenty minutes. From there within a few yards one reaches a monument built of large blocks of masonry and carved with lions. It is reputed to be the tomb of a Jew called Hyrcanus. Along the south side of the valley there are rock cut caves one of which has the name of Tobiah carved in Aramaic characters over the entrance.

JERASH and AJLUN

The motor road to Jerash branches off the Amman es-Salt road at Suweileh, 12 Kms. west of Amman, and passes through the plain of Biqa', with the Mountains of Gilead straight ahead to the north. Off the right of the road, 2 Kms. north of Suweileh, at Khirbat Safut are the ruins of a Byzantine Church dedicated to St. Macarius. 29 Kms. farther we cross the River Zerqa, the banks of which are lined with oleander bushes like Wadi Shu'eib, 7 Kms. beyond the Zerqa bring one to the imposing ruins of Jerash.

Main landmarks in the history of Jerash.

Circa 300 B.C.	Gerasa founded by the soldiers of Alexander the Great or of one of his successors and called Antiocheia on the Chrysoroas.
Circa 84 B.C.	Occupied for a short period by Alexander Jannaeus.
Circa 63 B.C.	Joined the Decapolis.
Circa A.D. 90.	Absorbed in the new Roman Province of Arabia.
A.D. 117-180.	Period of its greatness and height of its prosperity under the Antonines.
Circa A.D. 350.	Christianity gained a foothold in Gerasa.
A.D. 400-600.	Many churches built in Gerasa.
A.D. 634.	Captured by the Arabs and sinking slowly to obscurity.
A.D. 1878.	East half settled by Circassians.

The tour round the ruins of Jerash can be comfortably accomplished in one day. The visitor is advised to bring a sandwich lunch; soft drinks can be obtained in a nearby coffee house.

TRIUMPHAL ARCH JERASH

Before reaching the ancient city walls (going back to the First Century A.D.), we pass by the Triumphal Arch, a triple arcade to the west of the road, built to celebrate Hadrian's visit to the city in A.D. 129. Beyond this stands the ancient Hippodrome.

The city walls are still visible in parts. The present road passes over the substructure of the city walls east of the South Gate of the city, where entrance tickets at 100 fils (2/—) are obtained. The South Gate is another triple arcade, considerably smaller than the Triumphal Arch. To the left of it stands the South Temple dedicated to Zeus, built during the Second Century A.D., on the site of an earlier sanctuary. Further to the left is the South or Great Theatre containing 32 tiers of seats arranged in semicircles and facing the city. It was built during the First Century A.D. and it accommodated as many as 6000 spectators.

Proceeding north, the visitor reaches the Forum, an elliptical enclosure, colonnaded and paved with flagstones;

56 of the columns are still standing in their original positions.

Beyond the Forum, and running north-south was the main thoroughfare of Gerasa, crossing the city from the Forum to the North Gate. It was flanked on both sides by columns, some of which are still standing, and is at present known as the "Street of Columns". Crossing the street at right angles there are two other thoroughfares running east-west which have recently been cleared; at each of the cross roads there was a monument consisting of four piers, each of which supported four columns, which was probably surmounted by a statue. These are known as the Tetrapyla: the first or South Tetrapylon stood at the cross roads about 200 yards north of the Forum, and the second or North Tetrapylon at the cross roads 350 yards further north.

About 180 yards beyond the South Tetrapylon, on the left hand side of the Street of Columns is the Nymphaeum, a semicircular structure, which was both an ornamental fountain and a temple of the Nymphs (water sprites). Its walls are elaborately carved with fish, dolphins and other sea denizens.

Immediately after the Nymphaeum, on the same side of the street, stand the impressive ruins of the Temple of Artemis and its Propylaea or Gate (Second Century A.D.). On going through the massive Propylaea we come to a flight of stairs leading up to a platform. Beyond this there was a second flight of stairs (until recently mostly covered up or destroyed but at present, they are being cleared and repaired) running the whole width of the court-yard, which led up to the outer porch of the temple. This porch, like the porches of most Greek temples, consists of the outer wall of the courtyard with a row of columns in front of it. Five doors lead from the outer porch into the courtyard, which is a rectangular enclosure consisting

SOUTH OF GREAT THEATRE — JERASH

FORUM JERASH

STREET OF COLUMNS JERASH

of an outer wall with a row of columns running round the four sides, and forming with the outer wall a kind of portico. Abutting against the walls there were a series of rooms or recesses. In addition to the doors already mentioned, there is a door on the north and another on the south leading out of the courtyard.

In the middle of the courtyard stands the temple proper; it is approached by a flight of stairs which were unfortunately removed at some remote period. The cella, or holy part of the temple, was built on a platform or podium carried on vaults, and was surrounded on all four sides by a row of columns carrying Corinthian capitals. The cella itself is now blocked up; but the interior walls are plain, like the rest of the temple walls, except for the rectangular niches, which were faced with marble. In one of the vaults carrying the platform on which the temple stands is the Museum of Inscriptions, the key of which is kept by the guard.

This temple is the most imposing monument in Jerash, and no wonder, for Artemis was the patron goddess of the city.

Opposite the Temple of Artemis are the remains of the Viaduct Church, built over the forecourt of the temple which had a triple arcade, and which led up to the Propylaea of the Temple of Artemis, the intention being to give an open view of the Propylaea and temple from as great a distance as possible. The church is paved with a fine mosaic floor.

A few steps further along the Street of Columns bring us to the Baths, situated to the east of the street. These belong to the Second Century A.D. and contain the first example of a dome built directly on pendentives. On the other side of the street is the North or Small Theatre with a seating capacity for only 1200 spectators. It has been suggested that this theatre was reserved for gladiatorial and animal combats. 200 yards further along the same street bring us to the North Gate and so to the north limit of the city.

TEMPLE OF ARTEMIS JERASH

There are no less than thirteen churches at present visible at Jerash, and many more may lie buried under the ground. All the known churches are dated except one.

South of the Nymphaeum stood the Cathedral, the earliest Christian building known in Jerash. It is dated to A.D. 350-375 and consists of a central nave with north and south aisles, an apse at the east end of the nave and a chancel, separated from the nave by a screen. The architectural details, as well as the masonry, were mainly taken from the Temple of Dionysos.

West of the Cathedral lie the ruins of the large Church of St. Theodore built about A.D. 496. It was paved with slabs of marble and coloured limestone, but little of this pavement survives at present. Farther west are the ruins of three churches; the plan of the middle church, dedicated to St. John, consists of a circle set in a square, while the other two, the south dedicated to SS. Cosmas and Damianus, and the north to St. George, are of the usual basilica type, like the Cathedral. The three churches communicated with one another by doors and had one atrium in common. All three were paved with fine mosaic floors.

The church west of the Temple of Artemis was originally a synagogue which was converted into a church in A.D. 530. More ruined churches can be seen here and there, but they are not sufficiently important for the casual visitor to warrant detailed description. Those interested are advised to consult Gerasa, City of the Decapolis edited by Kraeling.

Outside the city walls, on the north, is the principal cemetery of the ancient city. Nearby is a spring called Birketein (the two pools), and a small theatre where the licentious water festival of Maiumas was held even as late as the Sixth Century A.D., as we learn from an inscription found in the theatre.

Ajlun lies 25.5 Kms. roughly north-west of Jerash. It contains a mosque with a minaret built during the Middle Ages on the site of a Christian church. Qal'at er Rabad, which stands on top of the mountain above Ajlun, was built by Izz ed Din Usama, one of the generals of Saladin, in A.D. 1184. It was destroyed in 1260 by the Mongols and rebuilt by the Mameluk Sultan Beybars. It is one of the few surviving examples of Saracenic military architecture of the Middle Ages and is well worth a visit.

AMMAN to PETRA

There are two alternative roads leading from Amman to Petra, both starting from the same point and over-lapping for a distance of about twenty kilometres.

After crossing the bridge over Wadi Amman in the south-west corner of the city in the Muhajirin Quarter, the road proceeds up-hill until it reaches the top of the Qatraneh Plateau, whence, it continues almost due south for a long distance. About twelve kilometres south of Amman the remains of an imposing Roman Mausoleum known as al Qasr, may be seen on the right. Eight kilometres further still, the road forks into two, one road branching off to the left and the other to the right. The first road runs straight to Ma'an, close to the railway line, via Jiza and Qatraneh where travellers report to the police. After Ma'an the road follows the road to Aqaba for a distance of about twenty kilometres until a sharp turn to the right is reached. Here, leaving the Aqaba road, the car follows the turn to the right, which leads straight to Ain Musa, the village of Al Ji and the entrance of Wadi Siq. The whole distance from Amman can be covered in less than four hours, but the way is devoid of interest and rather monotonous.

The second road continues to run due south after the fork. It is far more picturesque than the other road, but it takes three times as long to negotiate. Travellers taking this road are advised to start the trip to Petra at a very early hour in order to have ample time for short stops on the way, and in order to reach Petra before dusk. The traveller is further advised to take a picnic lunch with him including a copious supply of beverages to be taken on the way, as, apart from such things as eggs and fruit, it is almost impossible to procure any other food before he reaches Petra.

Twelve kilometres beyond the fork separating the two roads, the road passes through Madaba. A short distance after Madaba the road crosses the gorge of the Wala, a tributary of the Arnon. On the other side of the Wala and about thirty-two kilometres beyond Madaba, stand the ruins of Diban, the Biblical Dhibon. Diban has been excavated in recent years and an imposing city wall of the Nineth Century B.C. has been discovered.

Proceeding south from Diban one eventually reaches Kerak after crossing the deep gorge of the Arnon. The road from Madaba to Kerak passes through the most fertile land of Transjordan. In spring it becomes a vast carpet of beautiful wild flowers.

Kerak stands on a hill-top, about 70 Kms. south of Diban. Its principal monument is the Citadel or the Crusader Castle at the south-west corner of the city, separated from it by a fosse, now filled up. About thirty kilometres after Kerak we start crossing the picturesque Wadi el Hasa. On the other side of the Zered **Khirbat Tannur** looms on a hill-top to the west of the road. It is the site of a Nabataean temple, discovered and excavated by Dr. Nelson Glueck, formerly Director of the American School of Oriental Research in Jerusalem. Amongst other things discovered was a veiled figure of Atargatis, now in the Palestine Archaeological Museum in Jerusalem.

The road continues to rise from the ford over the Zered until the plateau is reached whence it runs south again as far as Tafileh. About 29 kilometres beyond Tafileh, at Dhana, a superb view is obtained of the Wadi Araba and the hills beyond. Fifteen kilometres beyond Dhana bring us to the turning on the right which leads to Shobak, the ancient Crusader fortress of Montreal.

FOUND IN خربة التنور 1936-37
تمثال عطار غاتس الربة الخصب

KHIRBAT TANNUR STATUE OF ATARGATIS

Shobak stands about twenty-six kilometres from the turning on the right hand side of the road; a modern village has sprung up within its walls, but an impressive view of the fortress is obtained from outside, the walls being still very well preserved.

The next stop after Shobak is Ain Musa (the spring of Moses) which lies at the cross roads of Shobak, Ma'an and Al Ji. Ain Musa is considered by the local inhabitants erroneously to be the traditional site of Mass and Meribah, where Moses smote the rock and water gushed forth (Exodus xvii, 1-7). A few more kilometres take us to Al Ji and the gorge of es Siq.

A third alternative way to reach Petra is to charter a plane from Amman to Ma'an and thence to hire a car to Petra. Tourist Agencies can generally arrange this for interested groups.

Cars are left at the entrance to the gorge of es Siq, and horses and pack mules hired. Here also entrance tickets may be obtained (J.D. 1.- per person). For the journey from this point to Petra and for the sightseeing trips at Petra, it is obligatory to engage local guides. This formality is generally arranged by the police.

The bridle path through es Siq to Petra is one of the most romantic experiences in the world. Here one enters a dream-like, unreal world. Soft sandstone cliffs of varied and unusual colours and fantastic shapes tower to a height of 200 to 300 feet, and appear almost to meet above the astonished traveller's head. It is a gorge straight out of fairyland, and although its general direction remains east-west, it winds and turns so bewilderingly that it is impossible to see more than a few yards ahead. One constantly expects the mythical creatures of one's childhood stories to appear around the next turn.

An aqueduct cut in the rock next to the path helps to disillusion the traveller and remind him every now and then, that he is not actually dreaming, but approaching an ancient city to which water supply was a constantly pressing problem. The grand moment comes when instead of meeting a goblin, Khaznat Far'on suddenly appears

KHAZNAT FAR'ON — PETRA

round a corner. This is an imposing tomb hewn out of "the rose red rock of Petra" in the late Greek style. One is staggered by the magnificence of this most perfectly preserved of all the monuments of Petra. The front is in two storeys. The lower storey consists of the portico of the tomb, which is surmounted by a gable, supported on an architrave resting on six large columns of the Corinthian Order (one of which has recently been restored). Between the first and second, and between the fifth and the sixth columns, counting from the left, the wall is carved in low relief with a man leading a horse by the bridle while a snake appears to charge him. The architrave over the columns is carved in low relief with winged gryphons and chalices, while the pediment of the gable over the central four columns is filled with floral designs and a defaced eagle. The gable is surmounted by the symbol of Isis, i.e. a disk set between two horns. The second storey consists of three distinct classical motifs separated by recesses in the rock. The middle motif is a "lantern" similar to the monument of Lysistrates in Athens, supporting an urn. The field between the two columns is occupied by a draped standing figure of Isis, holding a cornucopiae (horn of abundance) in her left hand and a sistrum in her right. On both sides of this central motif are two other classical motifs, each one of which consists of the end of a gable resting on two columns. The intercolumniation, as well as the walls of the recesses are decorated with standing Amazons, wearing short tunics and brandishing arms over their heads.

After the Khazneh the bridle path turns sharply towards the north-west, and in a few minutes Nazzal's Hotel is reached where welcome refreshments await the tired but amazed traveller.

Main landmarks in the history of Petra.

| 797-779 B.C. | The Rock Sela occupied by Amasiah King of Juda. |

EL HABIS WITH NAZZAL'S CAMP IN THE FOREGROUND PETRA

Circa 650 B.C.	Nabataeans pay tribute to Assyria.
312 B.C.	Antigonus Monophthalmos captures Petra, but is waylaid by the Nabataeans in a night attack and his army is destroyed.
312-63 B.C.	Nabataeans maintain independence and carve out an empire in the whole of Transjordan in spite of the Seleucid and the Maccabaean efforts to crush them.
63 B.C. - A.D. 106.	Autonomous but more or less dependent on Rome.
A.D. 106.	Nabataean Kingdom annexed by Rome and becomes part of the Roman Province of Arabia.

To adequately appreciate the splendour of the unique monuments of Petra one must spend at least two complete

QASR FAR'ON — PETRA

days on the site. Since the trip to Petra by the desert route has been reduced by half a day, it is possible now to start the excursions at Petra in the afternoon of the day of arrival. The following is a suggested programme for a visit lasting two complete days; suggestions for visits of longer duration are made at the appropriate places for those who are disposed and are able to follow them.

First Day Afternoon.

THE OBELISKS and THE HIGH PLACE

The visitor leaves the hotel and retraces his steps back to the Triumphal Arch and the paved road which he followed in the morning in his approach to Petra. The Triumphal Arch was erected in honour of Hadrian's visit to Petra in A.D. 129. The visitor goes past the theatre and al Khaznah and proceeds to climb up between the clefts in the rock. After an hour's climb he reaches Zibb Atuf, where the two obelisks cut out of the living rock meet his gaze. The obelisks stand on a flattened base; each obelisk measures over 20 ft. in height, and both were probably connected with some sort of ritual. On the opposite side stands the principal high place of Petra, which the local people call al Madhbah "the Altar". It consists of a platform, 45 ft. x 20 ft., hewn out of the rock surface, with an altar erected on the west side.

Descending the rock cut stairs south of the high place the traveller soon reaches Wadi Farasa. Here the rock face is carved with interesting designs; the lion in relief in particular is worth noting. Farther down is the Garden Tomb, near which there is a terrace with a cistern for storing water, hence the name. We next come to the large Statue Tomb to the left of the path. The facade of this tomb is decorated with three niches containing statues.

The middle statue represents a man wearing a tunic in high relief, while the side statues represent young men with their robes flowing behind them. Facing this tomb, is a large room decorated with a frieze in the Ionian style and provided with rock cut benches along the three sides. There may be some connection between this room and the tomb across the path. It is known as the Triclinium, or room of funerary meals.

Further examples of Nabataean tombs can be seen on the way down to the camp if the visitor returns by way of Zibb Far'on.

South of Wadi Farasa, at en Numeir, there are many ancient rock cut stairs leading to the shrine of the Nabataean King Obodas; this is a plain hall, with a niche at the far end in which a statue of the king was placed at one time.

The visitor to Petra spends his first night either in a room in the hotel in front of a huge outcrop of rose red rock, known as el Habis, pierced by many chambers hewn in the soft rock (or indeed, if he expresses the desire beforehand, he may sleep in one of these chambers), the ancient sepulchral chambers of the Nabataeans. The ancient walled city of Petra occupies precisely the site of the camp and the area around it.

Second Day Before Noon.

ED DEIR.

Taking the second wadi north of the camp we strike a path which leads up the Wadi ed Deir. About one third of the way up we pass by the Lion Tomb, the entrance of which is guarded by two lions carved in relief. A short path leads north to Kattar el Deir or el Hammam, a group of rock cut chambers which contain Christian inscriptions,

ED DEIR FRONT VIEW — PETRA

and one of which is marked with a cross. Below there is a spring from which water falls drop by drop into small reservoirs. Returning back to the path up Wadi ed Deir, part of which consists of stairs hewn in the rock, we soon reach the important monument of ed Deir, which, after al Khaznah, is the best preserved and the most imposing of the monuments of Petra. In style it is similar to al Khaznah, but it is not so lavishly decorated with carvings as that monument. It is probable that it was a temple rather than a tomb.

A hundred yards or so south of this monument an extensive view of Wadi Araba and Jabal Harun is obtained. At the summit of the latter is a shrine said to be the Tomb of Aron, according to local tradition. From here we return to the camp, retracing our steps along the same route as the way we came.

Second Day Afternoon.

TOMBS TO THE NORTH-EAST
and NORTH OF PETRA.

In the sides of Jabal Khubtha, north of the theatre, there are many tombs cut in the rock, which are of extreme interest. About a third of a mile north of the theatre is the famous Urn Tomb. The facade of this tomb is decorated in the Greek style with arcades, columns and capitals surmounted by an urn. The interior of the tomb was slightly modified by Jason, Bishop of Petra, in A.D. 447 when the tomb was converted into a church. North of it is the **Corinthian Tomb** which is decorated in the same style as the Khaznah but with none of its beauty or elegance. Next comes the **Palace Tomb,** the facade of which is decorated in imitation of a Roman palace. The rock not being sufficiently even in height, part of the top storey

PALACE TOMB — PETRA

was finished in masonry. It has been suggested that this was the tomb of the kings of Petra. Beyond this tomb is the **Tomb of Sextus Florentinus,** one of the Roman Governors of the Province of Arabia.

Note: The tombs which are decorated with carved obelisks or stepped ornaments are generally held to be pre-Roman, while those decorated in the Greek style are post-Roman.

On the hill above the Urn Tomb there are other examples of the high places of Petra. For those who are keen on visiting other tombs and who have ample time at their disposal, a visit to the tombs known as Mughr en Nasara to the north-east of the Florentine Tomb and the Turkmaniyeh Tomb to the north is recommended.

MONUMENTS NEAR NAZZAL'S HOTEL.

Immediately south of the hotel stands **Qasr Far'on** a temple of the First Century A.D. The exterior walls of this temple are decorated with a band of triglyphs and rosettes under a projecting cornice in the Hellenistic style. A little over a hundred yards east of the camp are the remains of a Triumphal Arch or Gateway, opening on to a road paved with flagstones which has been recently cleared. The Triumphal Arch consists of a triple arcade which leads into an enclosure which contained the ancient public buildings of Petra, viz. the baths and the market place to the south of Wadi Musa, which runs through the heart of Petra, and the gymnasium and the palace which lie to the north of it. This imposing Triumphal Arch is considered the earliest example of a monumental gateway in East Jordan, and is deemed by some archaeologists to be earlier than that of Jerash. The paved road over which the arch stands has been cleared in recent years. To the south of the Triumphal Arch are the ruins of the public baths of Petra which are so completely destroyed as to be almost indistinguishable. They contain amongst other things a fragment of a frieze representing a Nereid. Beyond the baths stood the market place, which consisted of extensive halls and galleries extending over an area 650 ft. in length and 110 ft. in width. One can well imagine the hustle and bustle that went on daily in this now ruined and neglected building, when teeming multitudes of tradesmen and merchants gathered from all over the Near East. In the angle formed by the baths and the market place are the ruins of a temple, which was surrounded at one time by a row of Corinthian columns. To the south of the market place a solitary column, called at present Zibb Far'on, bears evidence to the existence of a former building, probably a palace or a temple, which was surrounded by rows of columns, and of which this lone column remains to tell the tale. North of the market place, on the other side of the wadi, lie the ruins of a palace of the Byzantine Period (in Jordan 4th to 7th Century A.D.), and immediately west of this are the ruins of the gymnasium.

The ruins of the walled city of Petra have so far been treated rather sketchily, because indeed they are very sketchy themselves. Apart from Qasr Far'on and the Triumphal Arch, almost all the ancient monuments are razed to the ground.

Turning back to the east and following Wadi Musa, we come to the Great Theatre of Petra. The seats of this are hewn out of the living rock in 34 tiers. The square chambers which are seen at the back are earlier tombs, the facades of which had to be cut away when the theatre was cut in the rock.

Retracing our steps back to the camp for a short rest, we can later proceed up to the top of el Habis, the mass of rock immediately west of the camp, which dominates the city of Petra, as well as most of its ancient Necropolis: it was probably here that the Crusaders built a fortress later. Behind el Habis is Umm el Biyara, the probable site of Biblical Sela whence Amasiah flung the Edomites into the ravine below.

With this our short tour of the important monuments of Petra is concluded. The foregoing is not an attempt at describing the wonders of this once remarkable city. What has been attempted and it may be hoped achieved, is merely to enumerate the outstanding monuments of Petra, and help the visitor to identify them. No words however can express the beauty of the setting, or the varied hues and colours of the rock, mostly rose red, but broken by white green, blue, brown and other hues.

The return to Amman on the following day is made on horse-back up Wadi es Siq, as far as its entrance where motor cars await the returning visitors to take them back to Amman. From Al Ji to Ma'an the journey runs over undulating country, partly cultivated but mostly barren desert. Between Ma'an and Jiza the countryside is not very interesting, and does not bear comparison with the route through Wadi el Hasa as stated earlier; perhaps just as well, as the traveller will by now have taken as much as he can digest in comfort, and may well spend the journey back to Amman dreaming about the wonders of Petra and Wadi es Siq.

From Ma'an those who have the time and the inclination may proceed to Aqaba on the Red Sea. It is the site of the Solomonic port of Ezion Geber, excavated by Dr. Glueck, formerly Director of the American School of Oriental Research, and later of Ayla. Opposite the mainland in the Gulf of Aqaba is Jaziret Far'on (Pharaoh's Isle), on which the Crusaders built a fort, which they called Ile de Graye.

MADABA
MT. NEBO and MUSHATTA.

The road to Madaba starts at the south-west corner of the city and passes through the village of Yaduda. Madaba is built on the site of the Moabite city of Medeba (Numbers xxi, 30). Its present inhabitants are mostly Christian. The Greek Orthodox Church was built in 1880 on the site of a Byzantine Church which had a mosaic floor representing the map of Palestine (the famous Madaba map) with a bird's eye view of the principal cities. Part of this pavement is still preserved and may be seen by applying to the local priest; a small donation towards the maintenance of the church is generally appreciated.

Khirbat el Mukhayyat, the ancient town of Nebo, lies about five kilometres north-west of Madaba. It contains the remains, amongst other buildings, of several churches paved with mosaic floors. The first to be discovered, was one dedicated to SS. Lot and Procopius. An Arab house was built on the foundations of the church, which helped to keep it intact. The church consists of a central nave and two lateral aisles, in other words it was built on the basilica plan. The pavement in the nave is divided into two parts one consisting of 20 medallions, formed by vine branches, which enclose harvest vintage and hunting scenes. The third row of medallions from the altar is particularly worth noting; the first medallion represents a donkey carrying a load of grapes, the second, a man balancing a stick on his shoulder, the third, two women pressing grapes around a wine-press, and the fourth a man playing a flute. In the other part to the west of the nave there is an important mosaic floor representing an altar on both sides of which stands a bull facing it. In each of the four corners of the panel there is a pomegranate tree bearing fruits;

its branches spread their foliage towards the centre of the panel. The dedicatory inscriptions in front of the altar and at the south-east corner of the church indicate that the church was dedicated to SS. Lot and Procopius. The date of the church is not certain but it has tentatively been placed in the first half of the Seventh Century, between A.D. 614 and 636.

There are two other churches of some importance at el Mukhayyat, one situated below the Church of SS. Lot and Procopius, and the other in the centre of the ruin, on the hill where the acropolis once stood. They are both paved with mosaic floors in similar patterns, in other words medallions formed by acanthus leaves containing harvest vintage and hunting scenes. The central figure in the second row of medallions from the altar, in the first of these churches, is a representation of Earth. The second church, dedicated to St. George according to an inscription, contains an equestrian figure of St. George in one of the medallions. Unfortunately both these churches had to be covered up again for safety.

Jabal Siyagha 10 Kms. to the north-west of Madaba is the traditional site of Pisgah, whence Moses was allowed a glimpse of the Holy Land, which he was destined never to enter. Excavations carried out by the Franciscan Fathers under the direction of Father Saller have revealed the remains of a Byzantine Church of the Sixth Century, paved with mosaics.

From Madaba it is possible to drive over to **al Mushatta** by crossing the railway line at Jiza. Mushatta is a ruined Umayyad Palace of the Eighth Century. It is a square building each side of which measures 144 metres. Its walls are strengthened by no less than 23 round or half round towers, while the gate is set between two towers, each of which is half an octagon in plan. The facade of the palace on both sides of the Gateway as far as the first round tower, as well as the Gateway towers, is decorated with geometrical and floral patterns in relief enclosing some animal motifs. It is a great pity that the bulk of these interesting decorations was removed before 1914 to the Kaiser Fiederich Museum in Berlin. The decorations represent 22 triangles the sides of which are ornamented with tendrils; in the field of each triangle is a large rosette. Between each pair of triangles is a hexagon, the interior of which is ornamented with acanthus leaves.

The interior of the palace was never finished except for two buildings, one at the entrance and the other at the opposite end of the palace on the north side. The first building consists of a large hall from which smaller halls and rooms branch off. The other consists of a long hall with a moulded arch over the entrance (now fallen on the ground) completed at the opposite end by three semi-circular exedrae, like a Roman basilica. The main hall is flanked by several independent units, each consisting of a central hall and four rooms, two on each side. An apse in the south wall of the palace indicates that it was intended to build a mosque there.

MUKAWER.

About eighteen kilometres south of Madaba there is a village called Libb. From there a car track runs due west for about seventeen kilometres before reaching the ruins of Mukawer (ancient Machaeres) where Alexander Jannaeus built a palace, of which some walls can be detected here and there. It was at this palace that Herod Antipas beheaded John the Baptist. The site however should be visited more for the superb view across the Dead Sea obtained from there rather than for any imposing monuments.

THE ARAB PALACES
IN THE DESERT.

The Caliphs of the First Moslem Dynasty, the Umayyads, who had just come from the heart of Arabia and who were still desert lovers by instinct, but at the same time were not proof against the comforts of the Greek civilization as it was known in Syria and Palestine, sought to combine the two by building luxurious palaces in the midst of the desert. There are no less than half a dozen such palaces in Jordan alone. One, Mushatta, has already been described. Two others may be briefly described here viz. Quseir 'Amra and Qasr Kharrana.

Quseir 'Amra is a hunting lodge 50 miles east of Amman. It consists of three parallel vaulted halls with a darkroom at the end of each of the two lateral vaults for a mid-day siesta. East of these halls is a bath consisting of three rooms. Outside the building there is a deep well.

The walls of the building are decorated with paintings. In the middle hall there is a representation of the Caliph seated on his throne and surrounded by his retinue. On the west wall of the hall on the right is a picture of the Caliph resplendent in his glory, while behind him stand Chosroe, the Sassanian King, Caesar, the Byzantine Emperor, the Negus of Abyssinia, and Roderic the King of the Goths, with their titles or names written in Arabic and Greek above their heads. As Roderic was contemporary with Walid I, it has been possible to date the construction of the hunting lodge with some certainty. The remaining walls are decorated with paintings representing various subjects; one worth noting is that of a naked woman getting out of a bath; others include dancing slave girls, hunting scenes, people swimming or carpenters and black-

QUSEIR 'AMRA

QUSEIR 'AMRA

smiths practising their craft. In the domed room in the bath the signs of the zodiac are painted on the ceiling of the dome.

Qasr Kharrana lies 40 miles east of Amman, between this town and Quseir 'Amra; both can be visited in one trip. It is a moderately well preserved palace, measuring 36 m. in length and 35 m. in breadth. It is built of undressed stones and plastered. There is a round tower at each corner and a half round tower in the middle of the north, east and west sides. The entrance occupies the middle of the south side and is built between two quarter round towers. The palace is built in two storeys along the sides of a square open court. The ground floor consists of a number of dark halls and rooms, probably intended for animals and servants (or slaves), while the rooms of the first floor are well lit by various windows, opening on to the central court. The exterior walls are pierced by arrow slits only. Some of the walls are decorated with carved plaster, a craft which the Arabs learnt from the Sassanians.

Mention may be made of **Qasr el Azraq,** north-east of Quseir 'Amra, made famous as Lawrence's headquarters during the Great War (1914-1919) when leading the Arab Revolt, and **Qasr et Tuba,** 40 miles south-east of Amman, as other examples of Arab palaces.

UMM JIMAL.

Umm Jimal is an extensive ruin which lies off the Amman-Baghdad road, a few miles past Mafraq and can be reached from Amman in about 1¹/₂ hrs. The ruins are those of a walled city, covering an area of about 150 acres, built entirely of basalt, while masonry tombs lie a short distance outside the walls. The earliest remains are Nabataean and go back to the First Century B.C. or A.D., and the latest to the Sixth Century A.D.

The principal Nabataean monument is the small temple belonging to the First Century A.D., just inside the south gate on the west side. It consists of a cella facing north with two columns in front. No doubt other Nabataean buildings existed, but they were probably dismantled to make room and supply material for buildings of later periods.

The bulk of the monuments of Umm Jimal belong to the Roman Period. They include the City Walls and Gates, the reservoir and aqueducts, the Praetorium, the Barracks and last but not least 15 Christian Churches of the Byzantine Period.

The City Walls vary between 1.80 m. and 2.00 m. in thickness. In plan they are roughly rectangular. They are pierced by six gates, two gates on each of the west, south and east sides. The only monumental gate is on the west side. The others are plain arched openings, except one of the gates on the south side and one of the gates on the east side, which are flanked by towers.

The Gate of Commodus (A.D. 176-180). The north gate on the west side consists of two towers projecting beyond the city walls, and connected by two arches which spring from piers placed against the opposite faces of the towers. It bears a dedicatory inscription dating the Gate

to the joint reign of Marcus Aurelius and his son
Commodus. The name Commodus has been given to the
gate by H.C. Butler who first attempted a detailed plan of
Umm Jimal in 1905.

Water Supply. As their city lay in the midst of a
waterless desert, the primary concern of the inhabitants of
Umm Jimal was to collect and conserve every drop of
the scanty rain water that fell during the short winter
season; hence the numerous cisterns and reservoirs. The
main water supply came from the dam built across the
wadi running west of Umm Jimal at a point a few hundred
yards north-west of the city. From here it was brought
in an aqueduct which fed a great reservoir in the middle
of the city. The aqueduct entered the city wall through
a specially concealed water gate in the east wall. The
reservoir measures 40 m. x 30 m. in area and is partly cut
in the rock and partly built of masonry; stairs lead down
to the bottom of the reservoir at the south-west corner.
Of the other reservoirs, that near the south-west corner
of the city is worth noting.

The Public Buildings of Umm Jimal. Just inside the
Gate of Commodus is a large open space free from domestic
structures but containing a few monumental buildings.

1. The Praetorium or governors' office (dated
A.D. 371) lies between the two gates on the west side.
It consists of two buildings constructed along the north
and west sides of an open court. The North Building is
rectangular in plan. The door is in the middle of the
south side and opens on to an atrium with four columns.
The atrium is flanked by two large halls, while to the north
of these are five rooms, the three middle of which open
on to the atrium and each of the two end rooms opens
on to the adjoining large hall. At the east end there appear
to be remains of a kitchen and a bath. There is evidence
of a first floor.

2. The "Barracks" (Vth Cent.). Near the middle of the south wall of the city is the largest building of Umm Jimal. It is known locally as ed Deir "the monastery". The building is rectangular in plan with a projecting chapel on the east side, and consists of an open court with double rows of rooms on the west side and half of the east side, and single rows of rooms on the north, south and the remaining half of the east side. At the south-east corner there is a tower six storeys high. On the top storey there is a "balcony" on each side, and inside, the walls are incised with crosses and the names of the archangels are written in Greek. It has been suggested by Butler, that this is a belfry for a semanterium.

The chapel attached to the "barracks" is of the basilica type, with a square instead of a round presbyterium or sanctuary.

Originally built as barracks, according to Butler the building may have been later converted into a monastery, hence the modern Arabic name.

THE CHURCHES OF UMM JIMAL.

There are no less than 15 churches at Umm Jimal belonging to two different types; the basilicas and the hall churches. The basilicas consist of a central nave and two lateral aisles, separated by arcades running parallel to the axis of the church, and ending on the east side in three apses or square presbyteria, while the hall churches consist of a single nave with arches running transversely across the axis of the church.

The church of Julianos (A.D. 345) is an example of the "hall" type church. It lies between the Gate of Commodus and the north-west corner of the city. It consists of ten transverse bays with a round presbyterium at the east end. It is the earliest dated church known.

Other examples of this type of church are the churches of Masechos, at the south-east corner of the town, and the church lying to the south of it.

The Cathedral (A.D. 557) is an example of the basilica type of church. It stands in the open space or piazza in the middle of the town, between the two gates on the west side. It is the largest church in Umm Jimal.

The following are other examples of churches belonging to the basilica type:

The three churches at the south-west, the north and the north-west corners of the city.

The West Church lies outside the city walls, but for the sake of which the walls were extended to include it. It is the best preserved of all the churches of Umm Jimal.

Klaudianos Church which lies opposite the Gate of Commodus.

Numerianos Church which is situated north of the barracks in the open space.

The Double Church situated between the two gates on the east side, consists of two adjacent churches one to the north belonging to the basilica type and the other to the south of it to the "Hall" type.

The majority of the domestic houses of Umm Jimal consist of rooms grouped around an open court. Examples of these can be seen near the east city wall, near the Nabataean temple, and on both sides of the open space.

THE TOMBS AT UMM JIMAL.

If time permits, a visit should be made to at least two of the Tombs at Umm Jimal.

The Nabataean Tomb, situated a few hundred yards south-west of the city, consists of a flight stairs flanked by upright slabs, which lead down to a vestibule opening on to a chamber with 15 loculi on each side arranged in three rows one on top of the other, similar to the Tombs at Palmyra.

The Tomb of Sareidos lies north of the road to the west of Umm Jimal. It consists of a chamber with three loculi on the west side and two on each of the north and south sides arranged in four tiers.

BIBLIOGRAPHY

1. King Hussein: Uneasy Lies The Head.
2. Publications of the Princeton University: Archaeological Expeditions to Syria, 1904-5 and 1909. Division II Architecture Section A. Southern Syria by H.C. Butler.
3. Gerasa, City of Decapolis, edited by Kraeling.
4. L. Harding, Antiquities of Jordan.
5. Quarterly of the Department of Antiquities of Palestine, Vol. VII, by G. and A. Horsefield.
6. M. Rostovtzeff, Caravan Cities.
7. Leon de Laborde, Journey through Arabia Petrae
8. Creswell, Early Moslem Architecture, Part I.
9. Jaussen et Savignac, Mission Archéologique en Arabie, Vol. III.
10. Sir Alexander Kennedy, Petra, Its History and Monuments.
11. S. J. Saller O. F. M. The Memorial of Moses on Mt. Nebo.
12. Cabrol et Leclercq, Dictionnaire d'Archéologie Chrétienne et de Liturgie, Vol. 101 pp. 806-866.
13. The maps published by the Departments of Lands and Surveys, Transjordan and Palestine, 1939, 1.250.000.

List of Distances between Amman
and the Principal Monuments.

		Kms.
Jerusalem to Amman via Naur		88
Jerusalem to Amman via Allenby Bridge .		108
Amman to Allenby Bridge		62
,, ,, Es Salt		29.7
,, ,, Safut		15.750
,, ,, Jerash		48
,, ,, Ajlun, via Jerash		73.7
,, ,, Qal'at er Rabad via Jerash and Ajlun		77
,, ,, Qatraneh		100
,, ,, Kerak		132
,, ,, Petra, via Kerak, Tafileh, Shobak		298.6
,, ,, Petra, via Ma'an		265
,, ,, Aqaba, via Ma'an		337
,, ,, Madaba, via Yaduda		32
,, ,, Mt. Nebo		42
,, ,, Qasr el Mushatta		32
,, ,, Qasr el Azraq		110
,, ,, Qasr Kharrana		68
,, ,, Quseir 'Amra		80
,, ,, Mafraq		65
,, ,, Umm Jimal		83
Madaba to Qasr el Mushatta		25
Madaba to Muqawer		35

(5 miles = 8 kms. approximately.)

Arab Bank Ltd

LET THE ARAB BANK
BE YOUR GUIDE TO
THE ARAB MARKETS

Forty four years banking experience in the Arab World is available to banks and international businessmen. Special advantages include practical advice, exclusive commercial information and business contacts. With its sister organizations, the Arab Bank (Overseas) Limited in Zurich and Geneva, The Arab Bank A.G. in Frankfurt, The Arab Bank (Nigeria) Limited in Lagos, Kano, and Apapa and correspondents throughout the world, The Arab Bank offers complete banking services in the ever-growing area of the Middle East and internationally.

THE ARAB BANK LIMITED
Doyen of Middle East Banking
Management: Amman, Jordan

Capital & Reserves	15,658,404 JD
Deposits	146,628,799 JD
Total Assets	213,061,302 JD

as at 31st December, 1972
JD (Jordan Dinar) = U.S.$ 3.105

Arab Bank has branches in :

Abu Dhabi, Ajman, Bahrain, Dubai, Gaza, Jordan, Lebanon, Morocco, Qatar, Ras Alkhaima, Saudi Arabia, Sharjah, Tunisia, Yemen, Oman, United Kingdom.

Sister Institutions:

Arab Bank (Overseas) Ltd.
Switzerland: Zurich,
Geneva
Capital & Reserves :
S. Fr. 38,900,000

Arab Bank A.G.

West Germany: Frankfurt
(Main)
Capital: D.M. 5,000,000

Arab Bank (Nigeria) Limited
Nigeria : Lagos, Kano, Apapa
Cable Address : BANKARABI

THE PHILADELPHIA
ORIENTAL BAZAAR

RIGHT IN THE HEART OF THE
PHILADELPHIA CLUB AMMAN

LARGE VARIETY OF SOUVENIRS AND ANTIQUES

~~~~~~

OPEN FROM 9 A.M. TO 2 P.M.

~~~~~~

TEL. 25191   PHILADELPHIA HOTEL AMMAN

The
PHILADELPHIA POOL

Amman, Jordan

In Amman

*Enjoy a Refreshing Dip
in the Paradise Pool of
The Philadelphia Hotel*

*and afterwards try a
Tasty Snack or Beverage
on the pleasant Pool side Patio*

*Free admittance for residents
of The Philadelphia Hotel*

Holiday Inn

Opening Winter 1975

200 Rooms - Swimming Pool - Cocktail Lounge

Holiday Inn

AQABA JORDAN

Opening Winter 1974

110 Rooms - Swimming Pool - Cocktail Lounge

Banquet Hall - Patio - Coffee Shop

WELCOME TO JORDAN — الأردن يرحب بكم

ROYAL CROWN COLA — رويال كراون كولا

RC — أرسي

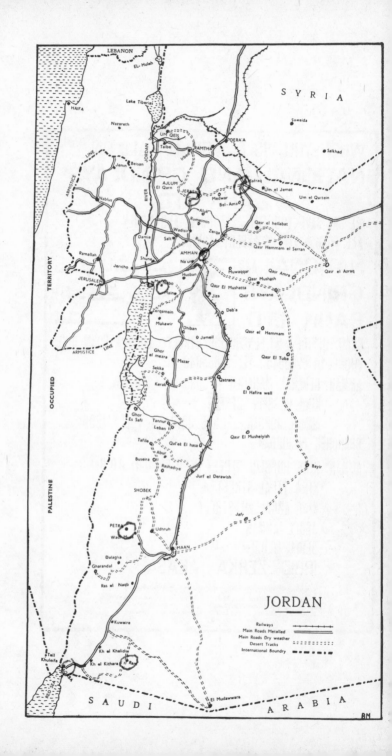

JORDAN

Railways
Main Roads Metalled
Main Roads Dry weather
Desert Tracks
International Boundry